A

CONVERSAZIONE

ON

MESMERISM AND PHRENO-MESMERISM,

BETWEEN

A MESMERIST AND AN ANTI-MESMERIST.

BY

THOMAS ADAIR,

HONORARY MEMBER OF THE SHEFFIELD PHRENOLOGICAL SOCIETY, MESMERIC
DEMONSTRATOR, ETC.

"This is Truth, though opposed to the Philosophy of Ages."—DR. GALL.

DUBLIN:

HODGES AND SMITH, GRAFTON-STREET,

BOOKSELLERS TO THE UNIVERSITY.

1845.

[Price One Shilling.]

A

CONVERSAZIONE

ON

MESMERISM AND PHRENO-MESMERISM,

BETWEEN

A MESMERIST AND AN ANTI-MESMERIST.

BY

THOMAS ADAIR,

HONORARY MEMBER OF THE SHEFFIELD PHRENOLOGICAL SOCIETY, MESMERIC
DEMONSTRATOR, ETC.

"This is Truth, though opposed to the Philosophy of Ages."—DR. GALL.

DUBLIN:

HODGES AND SMITH, GRAFTON-STREET,

BOOKSELLERS TO THE UNIVERSITY.

1845.

[*Price One Shilling.*]

DUBLIN :

PRINTED AT THE UNIVERSITY PRESS,

BY M. H. GILL.

INTRODUCTION.

————◆————

It is the custom with most writers to introduce their works to the public wrapped up in a long robe called a "Preface," but this the compiler of the following pages deems it right to avoid, because he is of opinion, that any publication worthy itself of attention, requires only very little introduction to recommend it. Instead, therefore, of delaying the reader with unnecessary details here, he begs of him to peruse what follows, merely intimating to him, that it is a brief history of Mesmerism, coupled with a number of well authenticated facts, simply and unpretendingly arranged in connexion with that extraordinary subject. Many of these facts, or others similar to them, have come within the Author's own observation as an experimenter and lecturer. They will be deemed improbable by those who never before heard of them, but the effects which Mesmerism is capable of producing may be said to be yet, in a great measure, unknown, and as they are of the utmost importance to the human family, the sooner that a knowledge of this science and of Phrenology shall become generally diffused, the better it will be for mankind. It was with a view of spreading this knowledge, that the following little work was, at the solicitations of a number of highly respectable persons, undertaken, and if it tend to produce inquiry about the subject of which it treats, or serve to dissipate any of the prejudices that prevail against that subject, the object of the Author will be attained, and his friends, as well as himself will be gratified. Hoping that it will be instrumental in doing both, he, without further remarks, bespeaks for it the consideration of the public.

A CONVERSAZIONE,

&c. &c.

--------◆--------

Mesmerist.—In the language of the immortal Shakespeare, I am led to say, that "there are more things in heaven and earth than are dreamed of in our philosophy;" perhaps you have heard or seen something of the beautiful phenomena evolved by Animal Magnetism, or, as it is commonly called, Mesmerism, and Phreno-Mesmerism.

Anti-Mesmerist.—I have both seen and heard a good deal about them of late. I look upon the whole as a piece of downright deception, imposture, collusion, and humbug, and all the professors and subjects of it as charlatans and impostors.

Mesmerist.—It is the easiest thing in the world to call any new discovery a downright deception, and the believers in it impostors, weak-headed charlatans, &c. Unfortunately this has been the language in common use, and the spirit evinced on the introduction of every new science in all ages of the world's history; look, for instance, at that which was used against Pythagoras, Socrates, Galileo, Newton, Bacon, Harvey, Jenner, &c., on introducing their splendid discoveries to the world; but allow me to say, that the employment of opprobrious language without argument, is indicative of a weak mind, for it bears no resemblance to the high-toned sentiments of a philosopher.

Anti-Mesmerist.—How is it we hear so much noise and talk about Mesmerism now, when no mention was made of it formerly?

Mesmerist.—Sir, it is quite evident to me that you are not much acquainted with the subject, so for your information, I may tell you that the principle called Animal Magnetism, or Mesmerism, is coeval with man's existance, and that the ancients were acquainted with, and employed it for the cure of disease, as can easily be shewn from history.

Anti-Mesmerist.—But pray, Mr. Mesmerist, where do you get your information? I shall be glad to hear a little more on the subject from you, although, pardon me, I do not believe a word of it.

Mesmerist.—Sir, " over incredulity is as much the evidence of a weak mind as too much credulity;" but as you seem disposed to listen, I will now proceed to shew you from numbers of authors, that the ancients were acquainted with what is called Mesmerism.

MAGNETISM AMONG THE EGYPTIANS.

Mesmerist.—Charlatans, according to Celsus, performed extraordinary cures by the mere *apposition of the hands*, and cured patients *by blowing*.

Arnobius, who confirms the same fact, states the reproaches which the Pagans addressed to Jesus in these words: " He is a magician," said they, " who has done all these things by a clandestine art ; he has furtively taken from the Egyptian temples the name of the powerful angels, and has robbed them of their ancient customs, their secret doctrines."

MAGNETISM AMONG THE HEBREWS.

The prophets of Israel, designated by the name of *seers*, were consulted as well for the ordinary events of life, as for sacred things. We read, for example, in the ninth chapter of the Book of Kings, that Saul went to consult Samuel, to learn from him what had become of his father's asses, which had been astray for several days.

Ahad, king of Israel, wishing to know if he should make war to take Ramoth in Gilead, assembled his prophets to the number of four hundred.

God speaks *during dreams* in the *visions* of the night, to warn man of the evil which he doeth, and to instruct him in that which he should know.

The son of the widow of Sarepta became sick, and his disease became so severe, that he no longer retained a breath of life. Elijah took the child in his arms, carried him into the apartment were he resided, and laid him on his bed. He then extended himself thrice over the child, measuring himself by his little body, and he cried out, " Lord, my God, grant I pray thee, that the soul of this child may re-enter his body:" and the child was restored to life.

In nearly the same manner Elisha cured the child of the Shunamite.

MAGNETISM AMONG THE GREEKS.

The Greeks had derived most of their customs from India and Egypt. Medicine with them was a species of priesthood, the mysteries of which the initiated could not reveal to the profane under pain of sacrilege. Thus we see the first Greek physicians employed, for the cure of their patients, certain *magic* processes, which can only be compared to the manipulations of the modern Mesmerist.

Pyrrhus, king of Epirus, cured persons suffering from spleen, by touching them slowly, and for a long time, on the painful side.

Aelin says, that on approaching the Psylle, persons were struck with stupor, as if they had drunk a soporific potion, and they continued deprived of their senses until the Psylle had left them.

The affections suffered by the body, says Hippocrates, the soul sees quite well with shut eyes.

According to Strabo, there was between Nepa and Fralea, a cavern consecrated to Pluto and Juno, in which the priests slept for the sake of the patients who came to consult them. Lastly, according to M. Foissac, the familiar spirit, the demon of Socrates, that interior voice, which apprized him of that which was to happen, and of that which he should do, was nothing but a state of crisis or of natural somnambulism, with which this godlike genius was frequently affected, whom M. Lebut has in vain sought to represent to us as labouring under insanity.

MAGNETISM AMONG THE ROMANS.

Esculapius delivered oracles *in a dream*, for the cure of his patients.

" I will not suffer persons," says Varro, " to deny that the Sibyl has given men good counsel during her life, and that she left after death predictions, which are still eagerly consulted on all difficult emergencies."

It is recorded in Saint Justin, " that the Sibyls spoke many great things with justice and truth, and that when the instinct which animated them ceased to exist, *they lost the recollections* of all they had declared."

According to Celsus, Asclepiades put to sleep, by *means of frictions*, those affected with frenzy. It happened even rather frequently, according to the same author, that too much friction might plunge the patient into a state of lethargy. These facts, to which several others might be added of a similar kind, leave no doubt with respect to their identity with the magnetic phenomena observed at the present day.

MAGNETISM AMONG THE GAULS.

There is not, probably, throughout all antiquity, a people among whom the power of Magnetism held more prominent station than among the Gauls. Women brought up and instructed by the Druids, delivered oracles, foretold the future, and cured diseases. The accounts given by Tacitus, Lampridius, and Vopiscus, regarding the Druids, bear testimony to the confidence they had in the accuracy of their predictions.

Endowed with extraordinary talents, they (the Druidesses) cured diseases deemed incurable, knew the future, and announced it to the people.

In conclusion, Pliny designates the Druids this way, in his description of prophets and physicians, " *Hoc genus valum medicorumque.*"

MAGNETISM IN THE MIDDLE AGES.

In all times, as well as in all countries, extraordinary things have passed for supernatural, from the moment they no longer admitted of explanation; and as it is natural to refer and attribute supernatural things to a divine power, the history of Magnetism in all ages, in the same way as in Pagan antiquity, and among the Gauls, is inextricably mixed up with the history of religion.

" The churches," observes M. Mialle, " succeeded the temples of the ancients, into which the traditions and processes of Magnetism were consigned. The same habits of passing whole nights in them, the same dreams, the same visions, the same cures. The true miracles performed on the tombs of saints, are recognised by characters, which it is not in the power of man to imitate; but we must exclude from the list of the ancient legends, a multitude of very extraordinary cures, where religion and faith interfered only so far as to produce dispositions eminently favourable to the natural action of Magnetism."

It is impossible for us, in a short discourse like this, to attempt a critical analysis of those dark records, and it would require a volume, merely to name the facts from the exorcisms of Saint Gregory Thaumaturgus, to the convulsionaries of Saint Medard. Indeed we may here observe, that some intelligent men, one hundred years before the *discovery* of Mesmer, expressed their objections to pretended miracles, and gave to magnetical facts their true interpretation. " Magnetism," says Van Helmont, " is active every where, and has nothing new but the name; it is a paradox only to those who ridicule every thing, and who attribute to the power of Satan whatever they are unable to explain."

Anti-Mesmerist.—This is all very fine, and to some may appear very plausible, but if such great and beneficial effects were produced, as you say, by the Egyptians, Hebrews, Grecians, Romans, Gauls, &c. how does it happen that this art was lost?

Mesmerist.—In point of fact it never was lost, it has been practised in all ages, and in all countries, although under no particular denomination,

Anti-Mesmerist.—Then how did it take that particular name, Mesmerism?

Mesmerist.—This name has been given to it in honour of Dr. Anthony Mesmer, a Swiss, who was born 5th of May, 1734, in a small town called Stein, on the banks of the Rhine. He obtained the degree of doctor at Vienna, under Professors Van Swieten and Haen, and having become acquainted with the virtues of Animal Magnetism, turned it to great advantage as a curative agent in Paris, whither he had repaired.

Anti-Mesmerist.—Was not this Mesmer you speak of a sort of visionary being, having written a book on the wonders and marvels of Astrology, and having attempted to demonstrate the influence the planets had upon the human body.

Mesmerist.—This may all be perfectly true, for in the writings of great men we often find error mixed up with truth. In his earliest years he evinced a great fondness for the study of nature; when a boy, his greatest pleasure was to retire into solitary spots, and there amuse himself in contemplating the operations of insects, the flight of birds, and in comparing the different shapes of plants, herbs, and mosses. He remained out in the fields all night, when the rising of the stars and the moon filled his mind with deep sacred things. " My mind was full," said he, " but I did not know what was working within me." This may appear rather visionary to some, but we perceive the early workings of a great mind. I have rather digressed, in thus giving you a short description of his earlier years.

Anti-Mesmerist.—How came the name of Animal Magnetism to be applied to this discovery?

Mesmerist.—Mesmer, the direct reviver of the system, being in the habit of using the mineral magnet in the cure of disease, at length discovered that it was by no means necessary, for by simply drawing, or making " passes" with his hands from the head to the lower extremities, he could produce powerful effects, and even influence his patients at a distance. From this time he gave it the name of Animal Magnetism.

Anti-Mesmerist.—Am I to understand that you agree in every particular with Mesmer's conduct?

Mesmerist.—I by no means wish you to understand that I agree with all Mesmer's conduct; he fell into a grievous error, by assuming that the healing power, whatever it might be, was resident in his own body alone, which in some measure brought down upon his head the indignation of the medical faculty.

Anti-Mesmerist.—Is it a fact, that Mesmer sold his secret of the art to each of his pupils for one hundred crowns a-head?

Mesmerist.—It is true that Mesmer had a great number of pupils, whom he instructed in the mysteries of his art, and no doubt but he received money for imparting his knowledge, but who would suppose that there was any thing wrong in Mesmer's conduct on that account? Has not every man a right to be paid for his labour and talent? Those who bring such flimsy accusations against Mesmer, may, perhaps, be guilty of worse actions themselves. But, to his credit, it is also stated of him, that he refused twenty thousand crowns from the King of France as a pension.

Anti-Mesmerist.—Was not Mesmer generally looked upon as a charlatan and impostor—some believing that he performed cures by concealed loadstones, others that he used some hidden electrical apparatus, Alchemists that he had found the philosopher's stone, and bigots affirming that he had a compact with his Satanic majesty, &c.?

Mesmerist.—This may be truer than any thing you have inquired of me yet. I doubt not but that such names and ideas were rife enough in Mesmer's days, and were unsparingly employed against him, but he paid little attention to these calumnies, and continued his practice with great success in Vienna. This of course excited the envy of the medical profession, for as soon as Mesmer had shaken the pecuniary interests of the Emperor's head physician, he was reported unfavourably of to the Emperor, and, being a foreigner, he was peremptorily ordered to quit Vienna within twenty-four hours, and to keep clear of His Majesty's dominions for ever. Indeed such was the fury of the faculty against Mesmer, that a law was passed, by which physicians and surgeons were prohibited from magnetising, under a penalty of forfeiting their license, and the profane were forbidden under a severe corporal punishment. This caused Mesmer to leave Vienna in 1777; but, after visiting Switzerland, the land of his birth, he made his appearance in Paris in 1779.

Anti-Mesmerist.—How was Mesmer and his novel system received in France?

Mesmerist.—The learned men of that capital had bent their views in quite an opposite direction; instead of finding support, he was laughed at as a dreamer; but his energy been untiring, he at length made a disciple of Dr. D'Eslon, a celebrated member of the faculty of Paris, and under the auspices of this physician, he published in 1779 his first memoir on Animal Magnetism.

Anti-Mesmerist.—Did Mesmer advance any theory, or attempt to explain the process or phenomena?

Mesmerist.—Mesmer gave the following theory, which to many minds appears, no doubt, a compound of truth and error.

MESMER'S THEORY.

" There is a reciprocal action and reaction between the planets, the earth, and animated nature.

" The means of operating this action and reaction is a most fine, subtle fluid, which penetrates every thing, and is capable of receiving and communicating all kinds of motions and impressions.

" This is brought about by mechanical, but, as yet, unknown laws.

" The reciprocal effects are analogous to the ebb and flow.

" The properties of matter, and of organization, depend upon reciprocal action.

" This fluid exercises an immediate action on the nerves, with which it embodies itself, and produces in the human body phenomena similar to those produced by the loadstone, that is, polarity and inclination. Hence the name of Animal Magnetism.

" This fluid flows with the greatest quickness from body to body, acts at a distance, and is reflected by the mirror like light; and it is strengthened and propagated by sound. There are animated bodies which exercise an action directly opposite to Animal Magnetism. Their presence alone is capable of destroying the effects of Magnetism. This power is also a positive power.

" By means of Animal Magnetism we can effect an immediate cure of the nervous diseases, and a mediate cure of all other disorders ; indeed it explains the action of the medicaments, and operates the crisis.

" The physician can discover by Magnetism, the manner of the most complicated diseases."

Anti-Mesmerist.—Now Sir, after such nonsense, you will surely admit, that Mesmer was only a "visionary dreamer;" and even supposing the whole of the phenomena which he produced to be genuine, he was by no means capable of introducing such an important discovery to the world.

Mesmerist.—No doubt but you may be disposed to quarrel with his theory, but Mesmer was not quite so visionary, after all, as you may think, for some of the brightest intellects have indulged in similar opinions; for instance, we gather from the writings of the immortal Dr. Jos. Gall, Dr. Bell, Paracelsus, Van Helmont, Santanelli, and Maxwell, that they believed in a magnetic fluid, which, they say, pervades the human frame and all nature: I will direct your attention to this part of the subject when speaking of Phreno-Mesmerism.

Anti-Mesmerist.—Did Mesmer meet with any other individuals, eminent in literature and science, who became convinced of his new delusion?

Mesmerist.—Amongst the most ardent and benevolent of Mesmer's followers were the Marquis of Puysegure, Caullet de Veaumorel, Petetin, Bergasse, Schelling, Von Humboldt, Ritter, Treviranus, Walther, Hufeland, Eschenmayor, Nasse;

Nees of Esenbeck, Francis Bader, Kieser, &c., all of whom devoted much attention to his discovery.

Anti-Mesmerist.—But, Sir, did not the French government issue a royal mandate, appointing a committee of the medical faculty of Paris, to investigate the new doctrine of Mesmer? And did not this same commission present a Report representing it as a complete delusion? And was not this Report a death blow to the pretensions of Mesmer?

Mesmerist.—So it was supposed, for it is true that the government of France ordered a commission of inquiry as you say, and an unfavourable report was presented; but one of the commission, Jussieu, the great botanist, investigated the subject for himself, and presented an entirely different view of the investigation; he drew up a favourable report, and adduced a great number of facts in its support.

Anti-Mesmerist.—You mention something about the Marquis de Puysegure becoming a convert. Pray how did that happen?

Mesmerist.—The Marquis attended Mesmer's lectures diligently, but was not converted, until one day calling at the house of his steward, he, by way of a joke, commenced the passes on his daughter; she in a very short time was thrown into a sleep, and the day following, the Marquis was equally successful in mesmerising the wife of his gamekeeper. Thus he became a convert, and one of the most successful mesmerists of the day; he was the first to discover somnambulism by the process, and at length published a work upon the subject, devoting besides, both on his estate and at Paris, much time to Mesmerism, for the cure of disease, in which he was eminently successful.

Anti-Mesmerist.—What did the Germans say to this? Did they still continue to prohibit the practice of Mesmerism?

Mesmerist.—By no means, although truth was crippled for a time, it soon burst forth in convincing splendour, and in an incredibly short time public lecturers on Mesmerism were appointed by the Prussian government in different universities. The same government established also an hospital for magnetic treatment, and sent the director of this establishment to Switzerland, to obtain from Mesmer all the necessary information.

Anti-Mesmerist.—I thought you had informed me that Mesmer was in France.

Mesmerist.—When the Revolution burst forth in that country, Mesmer left France, and retired to his native land, where he remained in quiet seclusion, pursuing his favourite science, and enjoying the rural recreation of cultivating a small estate.

Anti-Mesmerist.—And there, I suppose, he lived and died deserted.

Mesmerist.—By no means, he was visited by many eminent men, amongst whom was Professor Wolfart, who went specially to Frauenfield, to converse with the great Mesmer. Nor was this all, for a few years before his death, he had the satisfaction of seeing his works edited by one of the professors of the first universities in the world, and his science triumphant in Berlin, Jena, Bonn, Halle, Tubingen, St. Petersburg, Copenhagen, and in several towns of France, Holland, and Sweden —nay even in Vienna, where he was so badly treated, and where every attempt at reform is doomed to be crushed under the weight of absolute despotism—even in Vienna, in spite of the laws and law-givers, Animal Magnetism has performed, and is performing, the most wonderful cures. Dr. Malfati, one of the most talented and fashionable physicians in Vienna, adopted Mesmer's system, and practised it with great effect.

Anti-Mesmerist.—As far as I remember, it was prohibited in France, and the unfavourable Report of the commission had settled the question for ever in that country. Was it not so?

Mesmerist.—The French government ordered it to be confined to the medical faculty, after the Report of the first commission, but a second commission was appointed by the Royal Academy of Medicine in Paris, which, after much delay in investigating the subject, presented another Report in 1831. In this latter Report, a great amount of evidence was, to the surprise and mortification of a vast number of the medical faculty, adduced in support of the truth of Mesmerism. This evidence, together with many other interesting particulars, you will find in Teste's work on Mesmerism, translated into English by D. Spillan, M.D. of the Dublin College of Physicians. In fact, the first commission did not deny a great many of the truths which were presented; they merely disputed Mesmer's theory of a fluid, and attempted to account for the whole of the phenomena by attributing them to imagination, imitation, and touch; thus setting up one theory for the purpose of refuting another, and perhaps the latter more objectionable than the former.

Anti-Mesmerist.—If, as you say, Mesmerism is true, what benefit is society to receive from it?

Mesmerist.—In the language of Scripture, "much every way," for the cure of diseases, and for presenting to us a perfect knowledge of the working of the human mind.

Anti-Mesmerist.—Can you adduce any cases well authenticated, whereby it has been rendered useful as a curative agent?

Mesmerist.—Hundreds of cases are on record, and now I may entertain you with a few. " Dr. Wienhold, in Bremen, once treated magnetically Miss R., a young lady highly gifted, but entirely unacquainted with medicine. On one occasion, this lady prescribed, during somnambulism, the decoction of certain herbs, which she described most accurately, without knowing their botanical names. The herbs prescribed were not only unknown to the medical world, as possessing any antispasmodic or nervine properties, but even unknown also, as officinal, to all compounders of domestic medicine. Still the young lady persisted in demanding the decoction. The Doctor, looking at his Floras, thought that these herbs could not be found at that season of the year; upon making this observation, the somnambulist pointed out the very spot, about a mile and a half from town, where they would be found. The Doctor, in company with Obbers the great astronomer, went to the place designated, and to his great astonishment found the herbs. He collected them, and brought them, together with other herbs, bound in bundles, and presented them to the patient whilst in the magnetic sleep ; Miss R. chose among the different bundles those which contained the herbs which she required for the decoction. The same lady, upon another occasion, prescribed for herself a mixture. The Doctor fancied that the dose of crocus was too large ; he went to the chemist, and ordered the mixture according to the rules of art, diminishing the dose. The mixture was given to the patient while awake; she took it without knowing that she had prescribed it, and totally ignorant of its contents. The next day, when she had fallen into the magnetic sleep, she reproached the Doctor for his having acted contrary to her prescription, and insisted upon his obeying her orders. The Doctor then had the mixture made up as prescribed by the somnambulist, which, instead of injuring the patient, acted most beneficially.

The following is an extract from the Acts of the Philosophical Society of Berlin, of the 13th December, 1811.

Dr. Metzdorf, in Berlin, a physician, was called to a lady eighteen years of age, who was labouring under a severe illness. She complained of continued pains in the head, fits, want of appetite; she suffered from apprehension and melancholy, bordering on insanity; oppression in her chest, and want of respiration; her skin was dry and hot. These symptoms were aggravated by want of rest. The menstruation was irregular; the pulse hard and feverish; her bowels constipated. After having tried cathartics, and bitter tonics, and balsamics, after having endeavoured by all means to promote perspiration, in short, after having acted according to all the rules prescribed by the schools, the Doctor, at last, in despair, resolved to try the power of Animal Magnetism. He had never tried it before, and had but little faith in its efficacy. The young lady was altogether an unbeliever. The trial began on the 29th October, at twelve o'clock in the morning, in the presence of the mother and the sisters of the patient. After five minutes' manipulation, she found the pain diminishing; she felt heaviness in her eyes; the operation lasted ten minutes. After the departure of the Doctor she laid herself on a sofa, and slept an hour; she awoke with less pain than usual. During the night she had, for the first time, good rest since her illness. The next day the manipulations lasted for ten minutes, after which she fell asleep, and slept for two hours; the pains decreased, and she passed a good night.

On the third day, after having been manipulated at the usual hour for about ten minutes, she fell asleep, and slept for four hours; she awoke with but little headache, and with good appetite; her bowels had become regular.

The 1st of November the same favourable results from the manipulations, with the addition of gentle perspiration.

The Doctor was prevented, for two days running, from attending his patient, the consequences were convulsions, melancholy, dreadful headach, loss of appetite, and costiveness.

The 5th of November, at seven o'clock in the evening, the treatment was resumed. She complained of heaviness in the arms during the manipulations; excellent night's rest.

On the 6th the headach had diminished; the treatment was continued as before. After five minutes' manipulation she fell asleep, and slept an hour and a half, which was followed by abundant perspiration. Her appetite was restored, and costiveness removed; under the same treatment she continued to improve. On the eighth day she was not magnetized, and slept very little, and was restless; the ninth she awoke very weak, but got better after the magnetical operation.

The 10th; the treatment was painful to the patient, she felt a constriction in the whole body; she was unable to move a single limb, or even to speak; her facial muscles were convulsed; the treatment was continued longer than usual, and all these symptoms disappeared. After the manipulation she fell asleep, and awoke in the possession of her full health. No trace of convulsions, or of headach, remained; the melancholy had disappeared. The young lady left, that very evening, her sick chamber, visited some friends, and enjoyed, with liveliness, an impromptu dancing party, given to celebrate her recovery." The following case is also interesting:—

Madame Plaintain, sixty-four years of age, residing in the Rue St. Denis, consulted M. Cloquet about a cancer in the right breast, which she had for several years, and which was complicated with a considerable engorgement of the corresponding axillary glands. M. Chapelain, the physician of this lady, and who magnetized her several months since, with the intention, he said, of dispersing the engorgement of the breast, had been able to obtain no other result but a very profound sleep, during which the sensibility appeared totally abolished, the ideas retaining all their clearness. She proposed to M. Cloquet to operate during the time she was in the magnetic sleep. The latter, who considered the operation indispensable, consented to it, and it was determined that it should take place the following Sunday, April 12th, 1829. The two days immediately preceding this she was magnetized several times by M. Chapelain, who disposed her, when she was in the state of somnambulism, to endure the operation without fear, and who brought her even to discourse of it with ease, whilst, on awaking, she shuddered at the idea of it.

The day fixed for the operation, M. Cloquet, arriving at half past ten, A. M., found the patient dressed, sitting in an arm chair, in the attitude of a person who was tranquil and in a natural sleep. It was nearly an hour since she had returned from mass, which she was accustomed to hear every day at the same hour. M. Chapelain had put her into the magnetic sleep since her return; she spoke with considerable calmness of the operation she was about to undergo. Every thing being arranged for the operation, she undressed herself and sat upon a chair.

M. Chapelain supported the right arm; the left was allowed to hang down by her side. M. Pailloux, an *eleve interne* of the Hospital Saint Louis, was directed to present the instruments, and prepare the ligatures. A first incision, setting out from the hollow of the axilla, was carried above the tumour to the inner side of the mamma. The second, commencing at the same point, was carried below the tumour and continued so as to meet the first. M. Cloquet dissected the engorged glands cautiously, in consequence of the vicinity of the axillary artery, and extirpated the tumour. The operation lasted from ten to twelve minutes.

During all this time the patient continued to converse tranquilly with the operator, and gave not the least sign of sensibility; no movement in the limbs or *in the features*, no change *in the respiration*, nor *in the voice*, no emotion, even in the pulse, were observed. The patient continued in the state of indifference and of automatic impassibility, in which she was some minutes before the operation. There was no necessity for holding her, all that was required was to support her. A ligature was placed on the lateral thoracic artery, which was opened during the extraction of the glands. The wound was united by adhesive plasters and dressed, the patient was put to bed, still in a state of somnambulism, in which she was left for forty-eight hours.

One hour after the operation there appeared a slight hemorrhage, not attended, however, with any consequences. The first dressing was removed the following Tuesday, 14th; the wound was cleaned and dressed again; the patient evinced neither sensibility nor pain; the pulse retained its natural rhythm.

After this dressing M. Chapelain awoke his patient, whose somnambulism had lasted since one hour before the operation, that is to say, for two days. This lady did not appear to have any idea or feeling of what had passed; but on ascertaining that she had been operated on, and seeing her children around her, she evinced considerable emotion, which the magnetiser checked by immediately putting her to sleep.

Another successful case of amputation of the thigh, during the mesmeric sleep, without the knowledge of the patient, was read to the Royal Medical and Chirurgical Society of London, on Tuesday, the 22nd of November, 1842, by M. Topham, Esq., the gentleman who induced the mesmeric sleep on the patient. Those persons who have not ready means of seeing medical works, I would refer, for a full report of the cure alluded to, to Chambers' Edinburgh Journal, No. 572, Saturday, January 14th, 1843. It would be given here if it were not so long; the detail of it, however, would exclude other interesting cases with which I am anxious to present you; I may also direct your attention, for more cases of amputation during the mesmeric sleep, to the Zoist for October, 1845.

Besides these, a knowledge of which are within the reach of every one, I will give a few from the Alpine Philosopher, his work being scarce. The perfect cure, says he, of a disease was completed, which had baffled the skill of the medical art.

"Count B. S., fifty-eight years of age, of sanguine nervous constitution, a diplomatist and a man of letters, was spending his Christmas vacation with his family at his beautiful villa, on the Lake of Zurich. His happiness, however, was marred by a violent tic doloureux, the consequence of over-exertion in his political and literary pursuits. I was invited to spend the winter months with him in this chosen circle; and on my arrival I found the man, who otherwise was accustomed to electrify with his wit and humour a whole society, in the most pitiable state of irritability and pain. I asked the Countess what was the matter, and she told me that Dr. H., a most able physician and surgeon, was expected in the afternoon to cut the nerve which caused painful symptoms. "If the count will allow me to try magnetism, I can spare him the torture of the operation," said I to the Countess. "But he is not a believer in it," answered she; "and I have been the butt of his witticisms as often as I ventured to enter upon the subject. Nevertheless, we will try at dinner time if we can persuade him to allow you to operate." Several other ladies of the company agreed to turn the conversation at table upon magnetism, and to try to induce the Count to make a trial of it.

"The great diplomatist was conquered; after being assailed by the persuasion of his amiable lady and visitors, he resolved to submit to the experiment.

"The first half hour's calming treatment procured relief; after a fortnight, Count B. was so much improved that he began to acknowledge that it was an excellent remedy; the third week he was perfectly cured. No visible symptoms during the first fortnight, except now and then a contortion of the facial muscles, such as afflicted the late Lord Chancellor. During the three nights before his final recovery he had an abundant, I may say a flowing perspiration at the extremities. He has never been afflicted since."

A Case of Paralysis cured by Magnetism.—"Mr. B., a colonel in the Swiss regiment, forty-seven years old, in the best general health, of sanguine, nervous constitution, married, and having five children, came to Chur to be cured, if possible, by Mesmerism, of a paralysis which deprived him almost of the use of his left arm, hand, and leg, and which began to touch even the right side. The disease had begun nine or ten years before, but the patient could not say whether it originated in a fall from his horse, or from sleeping upon the damp ground during a campaign. I began the trial, and for sixty days there was no remarkable visible sign, no sleep, no heaviness, no warmth, no shivering, except on critical days, and by certain winds an increased movement of the affected part. The sixty-third day, however, he fell into a kind of epileptic fit, and fits more or less violent continued for twenty-seven days, after which a hemorrhoidal flux put an end to his disease. On his convalescence, he, for a month, made use of the battery, and was perfectly recovered.

"At the same time I cured two boys and one girl, all three crippled in their arms. These cases required but a few weeks, the patients not having previously wasted their vital powers by violent remedies."

Anti-Mesmerist.—You have given me a number of cases, but they appear nearly all to have taken place on the Continent. Pray, Sir, can you furnish me with any of those wonderful cures in England, Scotland, or Ireland; the cases you have just related reminds me very much of the quack doctor, whose cases of cures are generally performed a great distance from the locality where he is for the time being.

Mesmerist.—Sir, I can furnish you with more cases of cures by Mesmerism, and chiefly performed in England, Scotland, and Ireland, and all within the last six years, than you could read for the next three months; and, perhaps, before we part, I may entertain you by relating several which have come under my own observation, as well as many which have resulted from the experiments of others, who are engaged in the same good cause, some of them of the highest respectability and intelligence. I will also direct your attention to some works, where you will find a vast number of cases of cures recorded.

Anti-Mesmerist.—But before I take the trouble of reading these works, I would like to have an explanation of the case of the Okeys. Is it not generally believed that Dr. Elliotson of London was greatly imposed upon by these girls, and was not the whole affair exposed as a complete farce by Mr. Wakley, the Editor of the Lancet?

Mesmerist.—It is true that Mr. Wakley attempted to ridicule, and thought to expose Dr. Elliotson, but the latter answered the charge, and you will find his answer in the second part of his work on "Human Physiology," published in 1840, wherein he says, "that I should despise myself if I hesitated to declare my decided conviction of the truth of Mesmerism," and added, "just as I have stood abundant ridicule for advocating auscultation, phrenology, quinine, hydrocyanic acid, and creosote, and maintaining the liability of mankind to glanders, never having yet declared an opinion upon a new medical truth, that I had been obliged to retract, I will now stand more ridicule with the same firmness, and the silent pity and contempt which I have always felt for my opponents, till I see, as I shall, the truth of Mesmerism established.

"How I have up to this moment fulfilled my promise the world knows. I have now for three years carefully and dispassionately investigated the subject by experiments performed almost every day upon a vast variety of persons, and I not only report my firm conviction of the truth of Mesmerism, but of the truth of many points in it upon which I formerly gave no opinion, because I had not witnessed them, and was determined to remain neutral upon every point on which I myself did not witness facts."

Speaking of the Okeys, he goes on to say, in the work referred to. "The case of Elizabeth Okey, related at pp. 628, sq. 682, supra, has continued up to the present moment, and a sister rather younger than herself, taller, more robust, and of a bustling, hard-working character, who had also been treated by others and myself in vain for epilepsy, fell into a similar state as Elizabeth's, of ecstatic delirium, and was in this state when admitted into the hospital. When I first saw her she was in the delirium, but almost instantly fell asleep on my putting my finger on her forehead. The sleep was very short, but returned whenever I reapplied my finger. Her case likewise has continued up to this time. Scarcely a day has elapsed since in which Mr. Wood, who was my clinical clerk at the time they were in hospital, or myself, have not mesmerised one or both and carried on the investigation. We are enabled to state in the most positive manner, after the most rigorous daily observation for three years, that all the phenomena displayed are real; that the accusation of imposition is utterly false; and the report of one of them having been a performer among the Irvingites, or being an Irvingite, is, like every other respecting them, unfavourable to Mesmerism, a pure malicious invention of an unfeeling mind.

"These sisters exhibit perfect specimens of double consciousness; the most remarkable, perhaps, on record. In their ecstatic delirium, they know nothing of what has occurred in their natural state, they know not who they are, nor their ages, nor anything which they learned in their healthy state;

and in their natural state they are perfectly ignorant of all that has passed in their delirium. Their memory in their delirium reaches back only to the moment when each first woke from mesmeric sleep into the delirium. They would then indeed speak, but their minds were nearly blank, they knew nobody, nor the names, nature, nor use of any thing: they had to learn every thing afresh. For about twelve months, whatever was told them they believed, and whatever name was given to them for a thing, they invariably adopted. Not knowing what the terms father and mother meant, and the elder being told that I was their father, and Mr. Wood their mother, they always considered those words applicable to us only." For more lengthened detail, follow my former directions.

Anti-Mesmerist.—Now Mr. Mesmerist, as you have been very open, candid, and communicative respecting your art, can you by any means inform me how the mesmeric sleep, or any branch of the phenomena, is produced; this I wish to know, that I may try the experiment for myself, &c.?

Mesmerist.—Sir, there are various modes of operating, in order to induce the mesmeric states, and perhaps it may be as well to give you them separately; but before you commence operating, or allow any person to perform the operation upon you, let the operator be in perfect good health, and with sufficient experience to take off the influence that may be produced.

Anti-Mesmerist.—Are you aware of any bad effects resulting from it being performed by an unhealthy, or inexperienced person?

Mesmerist.—There have been some very bad effects produced by an undue exercise of the power, and much weakness and debility left after it. I remember hearing of a gentleman in the city of Carlisle, who attended the Author's lectures there, for the purpose of ridiculing them, but who, from what he saw, was made a convert of, and fancied he could perform the operation. Being on a visit at a farm house, a few miles from Carlisle, where the subject of Mesmerism became the topic of conversation, he said that he could produce mesmeric sleep; one of the servants was induced to sit for his manipulations, and soon became passive in his hands. But when, after having gone through several experiments, he attempted to demesmerise him; alas! the young man became to all appearance insane: this so alarmed the ignorant operator, that he immediately rode off to Carlisle for a druggist, who attended the Author's lectures diligently, and who became an expert mesmeriser under his tuition. This gentleman he took to the house where the young man was; operations were immediately commenced by him, the effects of the other's treatment dissipated, and the youth was restored to his proper senses.

A case of a somewhat similar nature occurred while the Author was in Dublin; several young men belonging to a printing establishment in that city attended his lectures, for the purpose of witnessing his experiments in Mesmerism. On going home, they commenced operations on each other; they at length found a young man susceptible of the influence, and by their undue exercise of the power, induced a state upon the youth, which made him appear as bordering on insanity; they became alarmed, but had the presence of mind to take him to the Author, who, after employing the necessary process, perfectly restored him.

Anti-Mesmerist.—Sir, according to your own words, it appears to me, that the experiment may be attended with danger, and therefore, it ought not to be practised, and it must in fact be wrong to do so.

Mesmerist.—It is a violation of the laws of both God and man, for individuals to be guilty of the conduct of incendiaries, in destroying property by fire, but does it follow, that we are not to employ such an agent for useful purposes? In point of fact, every thing in nature may be turned from its purposes; but the Deity has created nothing in vain; the elements He has placed within our reach, may all be properly used as well as abused, and what I wish to impress on you is, that the advantages derivable from Mesmerism counterbalance, in a thousand-fold degree, any evil that can be apprehended from it.

Anti-Mesmerist.—Sir, as you have promised to give me some idea of the practice of the art, will you be kind enough to do so?

Mesmerist.—I shall give you Delauze's method first. "Once you will be agreed, and determined to treat the matter seriously, remove from the patient all those persons who might occasion you any constraint; do not keep with you any but the necessary witnesses (only one if possible), and require of them not to interfere by any means in the processes which you employ, and in the effects which are the consequences of them, but to combine with you in doing good service to the patient. Manage so as to have neither too much heat nor cold, so that nothing may constrain the freedom of your movements, and take every precaution not to be interrupted during the sitting.

" Then take your patient, sit in the most convenient manner possible, and place yourself opposite to him or her, on a seat somewhat higher, so that his knees may be between your's, and that your feet may be beside his. First require of him to resign himself, to think of nothing, not to distract his mind in order to examine the effects he will experience, to banish every fear, to indulge in hope, and not to be uneasy or discouraged if the action of magnetism produce in him momentary pain. After matters are well adjusted, take his thumbs between your two fingers, so that the interior of your thumb may touch the interior of his, and fix your eyes on him. You will remain from two to five minutes in this position, or until you feel that an equal heat is established between his thumbs and yours. This being done, you will draw back your hands, separating them to the right and left, and turning them so that the inner surface may be on the outside, and you will raise them a little higher than the head; then you will place them on the two shoulders, you will leave them there for about a minute, and you will bring them back along the arms, as far as the ends of the fingers, slightly touching them. You will recommence this pass five or six times, turning away your hands, and separating them a little from the body, so as to re-ascend. You will then place your hands above the head; you will keep them there for a moment, and you will bring them down, passing in front of the face, at the distance of one or two inches, as far as the pit of the stomach; there you will stop for about two minutes, placing your thumbs on the pit of the stomach, and the other fingers below the ribs. Then you will descend slowly along the body as far as the knees, or better: and, if you can without incommoding yourself, to the extremity of the feet. You will repeat the same process during the greater part of the sitting; you will also approach the patient sometimes, so as to place your hands behind his shoulders, and let them descend slowly along the spine to the back, and from thence on to the haunches, and along the thighs, so far as the knees, or even the feet. After the first passes, you may dispense with placing the hands on the head, and make the subsequent passes on the arms."

The Author of this treatise generally stands or sits before the patient, gazes intently into the eyes, and causes the person operated upon to look steadily at him, and after the eyelids begin to droop he points his finger to them, and draws the passes over the head, begining at the cerebellum, moving over the coronal surface, and at the distance of about two inches, sometimes holding the hands behind and before the head; this process is necessary with some patients, in order that they may be passed from the first and second stages into the third, which I will have occasion to observe in another part. But there are various methods, and each magnetiser adopts his own plan, or that by which he can most influence his patients, which experience alone will teach. It often requires great concentration of the will to affect some individuals.

Anti-Mesmerist.—The cases you have given me are well calculated to stimulate me to make further inquiry, and your candour in communicating to me your mode of proceeding demands my thanks; but has not a plan different from your's, supposing it to be successful, been pursued by others; for instance, Doctor Braid of Manchester? What of him? Does he not disagree in theory with Mesmerists and Animal Magnetisers?

Mesmerist.—It is true that Mr. Braid does not believe in what is termed Animal Magnetism, and commonly called Mesmerism; but after a number of experiments, he has given to the state which he produces by his mode of operation, the name of Neuro-Hypnotism; this is of very little importance, for so long as Mr. Braid, or any other experimentalist, can induce a state in the human body, which tends to the removal of disease, it must be considered a blessing, and ought to be hailed by every benevolent mind with gratitude and thankfulness.

Anti-Mesmerist.—But what I want to know is, how he became acquainted with the subject, whether he has effected any good through his plan or not, and how he accounts for the effects he produces?

Mesmerist.—These facts I will proceed to give you. Mr. Braid first acquired a practical knowledge of Mesmerism from witnessing Lafontaine's experiments. The sleep produced by that gentleman on his patients arose, he, however, thought, from a fixation of the eye, not from Animal Magnetism. In accordance with this notion he devised a new theory on the subject, hoping that the public would be less prejudiced against it than against that of Mesmer, but the manner in which it was on its first enunciation received, shews that he as well as the Mesmerists did not escape unfair treatment.

In 1842, the British Association held their annual meeting at Manchester. On this occasion Mr. Braid presented a paper, in which he called the attention of the Medical Section to a subject not deemed unworthy the consideration of the Academy of Medicine at Paris. Far from receiving that courtesy to which he was fully entitled from his position as a man of superior intellect, however he might differ with the majority in opinion, Mr. Braid was subjected to the most contemptuous neglect, and his paper returned with every mark of indignity. To allow the public an apportunity of judging between Mr. Braid and the Association, the whole affair was taken up in an impartial manner by the *Manchester Times* of July 2nd, which journal excited no small degree of attention towards the subject. The subjoined, from the above-named journal, not only contains a justification of Mr. Braid, but also a description of a series of mesmeric cases of the most interesting nature :—

"We have learned, with some astonishment, that a paper, communicated by our townsman, Mr. Braid, has been returned to him under peculiar circumstances, and in a manner which, appearing to us as requiring some explanation, induced us to apply to Mr. Braid to ascertain the facts of the case. It is desirable that the members of the Association, generally, should be made acquainted before they separate, and it may be worth their while to inquire why the Committee took it upon themselves to declare, that a subject which had occupied the attention of many of the highest intellects in Manchester was ' unsuitable' to the deliberation of a body met for ' the advancement of science.' We understand that Mr. Braid intends to bring it before the members in a *conversazione*, to be held in a day or two. The following letter is his reply to our inquiry :—

"'TO THE EDITORS OF THE MANCHESTER TIMES.

"'GENTLEMEN,—In reply to your request, I have to state, that on the 18th ultimo, I sent a notice to the Secretaries of the British Association, that it was my intention to present a paper to the meeting here, on Neuro-hyponology. On the morning of last Wednesday I sent in my paper, entitled ' Practical Essay on the curative Agency of Neuro-hypnotism, by James Braid.' This was accompanied with a letter, requesting an early intimation of the day on which it was to be read, as it was my wish ' to bring up as many of the patients referred to as possible, that all present might have an opportunity of being satisfied, as to the facts not being exaggerated from the too sanguine expectation or bias of the operator.' I also intimated that, if they deemed it too long, it could easily be curtailed, if they signified their wish for me to do so. On Thursday evening, I was informed by Mr. Cottam, that it had been duly delivered to the Medical Section. I also inquired of a member of the Committee respecting it, but all I could learn was, that I should have an official announcement about it next day. However, none came. I therefore inquired of two other members of the Committee on Saturday, but both said they could not tell, and I must apply for information to the Secretary. I therefore addressed a note to the Secretaries, requesting to know when my paper was to be read. The only answer to this was, that, in about two hours after, my essay, and the letter which accompanied it, were sent to me by a porter, in an *open* envelope, not even accompanied by a note, but having an announcement on the outside of the cover, IN PENCIL, so that the porter who had carried it, or any, or all he might meet, might read the superscription, ' *Rejected by the Committee as* UNSUITABLE.' Such conduct I presume, requires no comment of mine to prove the *animus* of the Committee, or to point out their conduct in more glaring and odious colours, than the mere recital of the facts are calculated to excite in every honourable mind.

" ' I remain, Gentlemen, your's truly,

" ' JAMES BRAID.

" ' 3, *St. Peter's, Manchester*, 25th June, 1842.'

"Along with the letter above quoted, we," says *The Manchester Times*, " gave in our second edition, a few comments expressing our fear, that the rejection of Mr. Braid's paper by the Medical Section of the British Association, was in some measure the result of jealousy on the part of his professional brethren. We guarded ourselves against the supposition that we attributed the fault to the British Association as a body; we were more inclined to blame its rules, which placed in judgment upon the communications offered to the Medical Section, a preponderance of gentlemen who might possibly be Mr. Braid's rivals in practice. The Medical Section, as a body (though, with the exception of three names, they are all townsmen), may not deserve this imputation : the return of Mr. Braid's paper may have been the act of a portion, or if the act of the whole, it may be justifiable, for we will not condemn the Medical Section unheard; but still we say the rules of the British Association are at fault, in rendering those gentlemen liable to the *suspicion* of selfish and unworthy motives, and no such local preponderance appears in other committees. Mr. Braid's paper was a practical essay, not on Animal Magnetism, but on Neuro-hypnology as a *curative* agency, and he offered to produce patients before the Section, to prove its extraordinary curative powers. What could be a more fit subject to bring before an Association having for its object the advancement of science, and the investigation of the phenomena brought to light by those engaged in the different walks of science, with a view to rendering them applicable to useful purposes, we are at a loss to conceive.

"The Medical Section may be able to shew that we are wrong, but till then we are convinced, that the *Public* will be of our opinion, as we know a great portion of the very members of the British Association are; for whilst the doors of the Section itself were closed to Mr. Braid, the *elite* of the distinguished strangers were daily crowding his drawing-rooms and *conversazione*, with the most anxious curiosity to witness and judge for themselves respecting the merits of his discovery. We may mention as amongst these visitors:—

"Sir David Brewster; Sir Howard Elphinstone; Sir Oswald Mosley; Sir Charles Lemon; Sir William Jardine; the Rev. Professor Buckland, D.D., F.R.S., &c. (Oxford); Dr. Hodgkin; Dr. Stranger (the African traveller); the Hon. and Rev. the Dean of Manchester; Marquis Sauli; Colonel Wemyss; James Heath Leigh, Esq.; Captain Brown; Captain Pringle; Captain Rutherford; Lieutenant Frith; Lieutenant Macarlie; Joseph Corbett, Esq.; Arthur Strickland, Esq.; H. E. Strickland, Esq.; George Clarke, Esq.; Thomas Townsend, Esq.; Dr. Daubeny; Dr. Diffenbach; Dr. Hibbert Ware; Dr. Spencer; Dr. Richardson; Dr. Clay; Richard Taylor, Esq.; A. Booth, Esq.; Laurence Buchan, Esq.; Major Christie; Rev. George Eaton; Rev. C. D. Wray; A. F. Halliburton, Esq.; John Roley, Esq.; John Graham, Esq.; Professor Graham; Rev. William Bentley; Eaton Hodgkinson, Esq.; Roderick Impie Murchison, Esq.; J. A. Knipe, Esq.; P. F. Willert, Esq.; William Jordan, Esq.; James Hulme, Esq.; Jephtha Pacey, Esq.; William Joynson, Esq.; Robert Patterson, Esq. (Belfast); J. E. Oldham, Esq.; Robert Hampson, Esq.; Ralph Thicknesse, Esq.; W. H. Talbot, Esq.; —— Bailey, Esq.; G. W. Wood, Esq., M.P.; Dr. Roget; Dr. G. Lloyd; Dr. Lankester; Professor Henslow; C. C. Babbington, Esq.; —— Smith, Esq. (Deanstown), and J. A. Knipe, Esq.

"These facts speak sufficiently for themselves, we trust, as to the utter impossibility of stifling public inquiry, and with these remarks we pass on to notice the *conversazione*, given by Mr. Braid in the Wellington Room, Peter-street, on Wednesday, at noon. The *conversazione* was advertised by placard, inviting the attendance of the public, and of members of the Association. That the members of the Association availed themselves extensively of the privilege we can testify from personal observation; and by five minutes past twelve o'clock, when Mr. Braid entered the room, one of the most respectable audiences we ever witnessed in Manchester was assembled. The number present, as counted at this time, was upwards of 500, and in the progress of the proceeding swelled to nearly 1,000.

"Mr. Braid was received with great applause, and on mounting the platform he took from his pocket ' the rejected essay,' amidst renewed applause. It is not our intention to accompany him through his address, because we have before given to our readers Mr. B.'s theory of the cause of the interesting phenomena, which he calls Neuro-hypnology, or the rationale of nervous sleep. He detailed the circumstances under which he was first led to investigate these phenomena; the statement given above, in his letter, of the objection to his paper by the Medical Section; and observed, that the animosity of the *Committee* of the Medical Section, or those members of it who had influenced its decision in respect to his communication, was shewn in the suppression of all allusion to it in their list of ' papers offered to the section,' which was published on the first day of meeting. He had sent in his paper on the Wednesday morning; on the following morning they issued a publication, professing to name *all* the papers *offered* to the Association, to be read during its sessions; but though his announcement was given a month before, not only was *his* paper *designed from the very first to be rejected*, but the very mention of it among those *offered*, was suppressed. [Hear, hear.] His opponents had not been content with that; for when he had made known his intention to give this *conversazione* to the members of the Association, they carried their discourtesy and hostility so far, as to *tear down his placards* (*which had been sent for the various section rooms*), *in which the invitation was conveyed.* [Cries of " shame."] When he (Mr. Braid), first offered his paper to the Medical Section, he was aware that one of its most influential members would be influenced by no friendly motives towards him, because, from what had passed between them, he (Mr. Braid) had refused for six years to meet him professionally in consultation; but he had hoped there would be sufficient honesty of purpose at the board, to stifle private resentment, and defeat private pique. To say his paper was *unsuitable*, because of any thing in its form, was a misnomer, because he had offered to shape it in whatever way the committee thought most suitable: the only ground of *rejection* was unsuitable. But would the public believe this?   What, could it believed for a moment, that a subject which professed to develope a new and important curative agency, was unsuited to the inquiries of a body of the faculty, professedly met in their peculiar section for the advancement of truth?   [Hear, hear.]

" If its pretensions were just, why should they not be heard and acknowledged, in order that suffering humanity might, as widely as possible, be benefited by its being brought into the most extensive practice? If its pretensions were unfounded, why should they be afraid to put them to the test? [Hear, hear.] It was as much the duty, he contended, of an Association professing to have or its object the advancement of science to repudiate and put the public on their guard against any false impressions and assumed discoveries, if any such were offered to them, by thoroughly investigating the facts, as it was their duty to acknowledge real discoveries, and send them forth with the stamp of their approbation.   [Applause.]

" Mr. Braid then proceeded to read the rejected essay amidst considerable applause.   He afterwards mentioned some of the cures effected by this agency; and among the most striking was one effected on Miss Collins, a young lady residing at Newark, whose father, after submitting her to the treatment of the most eminent medical man he could find in that neighbourhood, took her to Sir Benjamin Brodie, in London, but she derived no benefit.   A spasmodic affection had drawn her head down close upon her shoulder, and she had been unable to remove it for six months.   By means of this agency he had been enabled to restore her in a few days, and she was now as well as any lady in the room.   [Applause.] He had a letter in his pocket from her father to that effect, and he asked if this was a subject unfit to engage the attention of medical men? [Applause.]

" As the company now became anxious to witness some of Mr. Braid's experiments, he proceeded to gratify them.   On the motion of Thomas Townsend, Esq., George Clarke, Esq., was called to the chair, and said, that having witnessed some of the phenomena of this agency, at Mr. Braid's own house, he thought the investigation of the subject a matter of importance to, and one which very much concerned the community, inasmuch as he conceived it was a very powerful one either for good or evil, and the sooner it was determined whether there was any imposture about the matter the better.   At the same time he begged to be understood as saying that he never was more certain of the honesty of purpose of any gentleman in his life, than he was of Mr. Braid's.   [Applause.]

"Mr. Braid now produced a patient who had come forward at his lecture at Macclesfield, and who at that time had lost the use of his arm, owing to a spinal affection, which had resisted every application of the ordinary medical description to afford relief. This man had received relief from this agency in the course of five minutes. Somnolency was now produced, and then rigidity of the limbs, by extending them so as to call the muscles into play. Mr. Braid then shewed several of his patients, one of them, an elderly female, said her name was Stowe, and stated that she lived at No. 1, Bank-place: this lady said she had not been able to see for twenty-two years without the aid of glasses, but by means of this agency her sight had been completely restored, and she could do needlework, threading the needle herself, ever since the first operation. The daughter stated that she had worn spectacles two years, and had derived similar benefits from Mr. Braid's treatment. She had also been entirely and speedily cured, by this agency, of a complication of diseases, pronounced incurable by one of the highest in office in the Medical Section.

"A man who gave his address ' Peter Hempson, Bank Parade, Salford,' came forward, and it was stated that he was suffering violently from rheumatism when Mr. Braid visited him, and was confined to his bed; he had received great relief in a few minutes from this agency, and in a few days was entirely well. [Applause.]

Thomas Morris, 6, Berkeley-street, Strangeways, who had been subject to paralysis for fifteen years, came forward, and though a short time since he could not move without two sticks, he was considerably better, and walked across the room without support in a few minutes after the first operation.

"Sarah Mellor, Chadderton Mill, near Oldham, who had suffered severely from a contraction of the legs, was introduced, and stated that though before Mr. Braid attended her she had to be lifted about, or use crutches, for nine months, she was now so far improved as to be able to walk, and was gradually recovering."

After this who will deny the use and value of such an important agency? A vast number of more cases might be cited from Mr. Braid's work on the subject, where he states, that he has extracted teeth without the patient feeling any pain. He has also cured deafness, tic douloureux, paralysis of sense and motion, rheumatism, ten cases, headach, spinal irritation, palpitation of the heart, diseases of the skin, tonic spasm. "I am quite certain," observes Mr. Braid, "that hypnotism is capable of throwing a patient into that state, in which he shall

be entirely unconscious of the pain of a surgical operation, or
of greatly moderating it, according to the time allowed and
mode of management resorted to."

Anti-Mesmerist.—Touching his plan, something is said
in the foregoing interesting lecture. Are you in any way
acquainted with it? if so, be kind enough to furnish me
with a condensed sketch.

Mesmerist.—As far as my memory will guide me, I will give
you some idea of Mr. Braid's plan, but my observations must
be very brief. " Take any bright object," says he " (I generally use my lancet case), between the thumb and fore and middle fingers of the left hand; hold it from about eight to fifteen
inches from the eyes, at such a position above the forehead as
may be necessary to produce the greatest possible strain upon
the eyes and eyelids, and enable the patient to maintain a steady
fixed stare at the object. The patient must be made to understand that he is to keep the eyes steadily fixed on the object.
It will be observed that, owing to the consensual adjustment
of the eyes, the pupils will be at first contracted, they will
shortly begin to dilate, and after they have done so to a considerable extent, and have assumed a very wavy motion, if the
fore and middle fingers of the right hand, extended and a little separated, are carried from the object towards the eyes,
most probably the eyelids will close involuntarily, with a vibra-
tory motion. If this is not the case, or the patient allows the
eyeballs to move, desire him to begin again, giving him to understand that he is to allow the eyelids to close when the fingers
are again carried towards the eyes, but that the eyeballs must
be kept fixed in the same position, and the mind riveted to
the one idea of the object held above the eyes, &c., &c. See
Mr. Braid's work.

Anti-Mesmerist.—What is your opinion with respect to Dr.
Braid's plan?

Mesmerist.—I doubt not but a state of sleep may be induced
by his method, but I think, as Dr. Elliotson very justly observes, that " Hypnotism is evidently coarse Mesmerism," and
my experience in a number of cases leads me also to believe, that
the will of the Mesmeriser has much to do with the operation,
but unfortunately this branch of the subject has as yet been
little studied, and is almost lost sight of..

Anti-Mesmerist.—I must now confess, that you have adduced
such an amount of credible witnesses in favour of Mesmerism, that I begin to think there is some truth in it, and that,
those men whom you name cannot all be deceived or be de-

ceivers; can you give me any idea of the state produced by mesmeric sleep?

Mesmerist. — Mr. Colquhoun of Edinburgh, who became acquainted with the subject in rather a curious manner, gives at great length, not only a full detail of the different plans adopted, but also the various effects produced, in what may be termed each stage or degree of the sleep.

" The magnetic treatment is usually administered with the hand, and is thence called manipulation. The usual method is to stroke repeatedly, with the palms of the hands and the fingers, in one direction, downwards, from the head to the feet; and in returning, to throw the hands round in a semicircle, turning the palms outwards, in order not to disturb the effects of the direct stroke. To magnetise in the contrary direction, that is, from the feet upwards towards the head, not only counteracts the effects of the former method, but frequently operates of itself prejudicially, especially in the case of irritable subjects. If we attempt to operate with the back of the hand, no effect whatever, will probably be produced upon the patient.

" If, in the course of this process, the hands or fingers of the operator are made actually to touch the body of the patient, it is called manipulation *with contact;* if, on the contrary, the operation is conducted at some distance, it is called manipulation *in distans.* The manipulation with contact is of two kinds; it is accompanied either with considerable pressure, or with light touching—manipulation with *strong* or with *light* contact. The manipulation with strong contact is certainly the most ancient and the most universally prevalent mode of operating." And, as I have observed before, traces of this mode of operating are to be found in almost all ages and countries. In manipulating with light contact, the hand, indeed, is conducted very lightly along the body of the patient; but the magnetiser must perform this operation with the utmost energy, and always have the desire of applying strong pressure to the body of the patient.

The manipulation *in distans* is applied at a distance of generally from two to six inches from the patient's body; in the case of very susceptible persons it is performed at a still greater distance. The effects of this mode of manipulating are less intense than those produced by actual contact, and, besides, it requires a greater energy of volition on the part of the magnetiser. It is, however, frequently employed in magnetising very irritable patients, who cannot endure any strong method. Much, of course, must depend upon the skill and judgment of the magnetiser, who will vary his modes of operating according to the effects produced, and the degree of sensibility exhibited by the patient.

"Before commencing the magnetic manipulations, it is necessary that both the magnetiser and the patient should be conveniently placed; in order that the former may be enabled freely to perform his operations, and the latter prepared for the expected crisis of sleep. A semi-recumbent posture of the patient is, upon the whole, the most convenient, the body being, at the same time, so far bent, that the operator can reach, without difficulty, from the crown of the head to the toes. Should the patient be unable to leave his bed, we must endeavour to place him in a proper bending position by means of pillows. It is not necessary that the patient should be completely undressed, only no silk covering should be allowed to intervene.

"The best situation, perhaps, in which a magnetic patient can be placed, is in an easy arm-chair, with his hands resting on the arms, his feet upon a foot-stool, and his knees bent somewhat forward. The magnetizer then places himself upon a common chair, opposite to the patient, and so near as to be able to enclose his knees within his own, but without designedly touching them.

"The effects produced by Animal Magnetism upon the organism of the patients is truly wonderful, and can scarcely be expected to obtain belief, excepting from those who have actually experienced or witnessed them. These effects are very various, and may be divided into two classes. The first consists of those general effects which are produced upon the entire bodily frame, and which are not merely periodical, but continue throughout the whole treatment. The second comprehends those which affect only some particular functions of the organization, and which are not constantly manifested, but only at certain times, and especially during the magnetic manipulations. These last may be reckoned among the particular effects of Animal Magnetism.

"The general effects of *Animal Magnetism*, which may be regarded as permanent states of the organization, and which always manifest themselves, in a greater or less degree, in all subjects whose diseases are of such a nature as to admit of the application of this treatment, and which, therefore, seem to originate from the sympathy of the whole body, are chiefly the following :

"I. A general excitement and strengthening of the vital functions, without any considerable *stimulus* in the nervous, muscular, vascular, and digestive organs. Persons who could not be strengthened by corroborant medicines of any kind, have been restored to health, from a state of the greatest debility, in a short time, by means of the magnetic treatment. The application of this remedy quickens the pulse, produces an increased degree of warmth, greater sensitive powers, and mental cheerfulness. The appetite and the digestion are increased; the bowels, which had previously been kept open by artificial means, now become regular, and the patient acquires a liking for such kinds of food as are good for him, and an aversion from such as are injurious. *Animal Magnetism* also promotes all the other secretions. In those complaints which are peculiar to females, it is said to be the most powerful and effectual remedy hitherto discovered. It seems to operate principally upon the great concatenation of sympathetic nerves situated in the abdomen, and, by means of their various combinations, to communicate its influence to the rest of the system.

"II. It affords a gentle *stimulus*, pervading, generally, the whole surface of the body, by which all disturbed harmony and diseased local action are removed, and the *equilibrium* again restored. In this way *Animal Magnetism* soothes the most violent action of the nervous system, the tumult of the muscles, and the over-exertion of the vital functions in the whole economy.

"III. It draws off the increased vital action from the diseased parts, and conducts it to others. By this means, a two-fold advantage is obtained. In the first place, the excited action is carried away from the internal and more noble organs, to such whose violent action is attended with less injury to the system; and, in the second place, the salutary vital action is strengthened and increased, particularly in the debilitated. The consequences of the magnetic treatment, therefore, are *soothing* and strengthening. In most instances, the agitation produced by the diseased organization is gradually allayed, until at length a perfect recovery is effected.

"IV. Animal Magnetism occasions a diminution, and total removal of the existing cause of the diseased action of the nervous system.

"The particular effects of Animal Magnetism, which are not the necessary consequences of its application, but which only occasionally manifest themselves, periodically, in a greater or less degree, in individual cases, are exceedingly various, and seem to depend, in a great measure, upon the peculiar physical and moral constitution, not only of the patient, but of the operating magnetiser.

" The *first* degree presents no remarkable phenomena. The intellect and the senses still retain their usual powers and susceptibilities.   For this reason, the first degree has been denominated the degree of *waking.*

" In the *second* degree, most of the senses still remain in a state of activity. That of vision only is impaired; the eye withdrawing itself gradually from the power of the will. This second degree, in which the sensibility is partially disturbed, is by some magnetisers called the *half sleep* or the *imperfect* crisis.

"In the *third* degree, the whole of the organs through the medium of which our correspondence with the external world is carried on (the senses), refuse to perform their respective functions, and the patient is placed in that unconscious state of existence, which is called the magnetic sleep.

" In the *fourth degree*, the patient awakes, as it were, within himself, and his consciousness return. He is in a state which can neither be called sleeping nor waking, but which appears to be something between the two. When in this state, he is again placed in a very peculiar connexion with the external world. This fourth degree has been distinguished, in the writings of the Animal Magnetisers, by the name of the *perfect crisis* or *simple somnambulism.*

" In the *fifth* degree the patient is placed in what is called the state of *self*-intuition. When in this state, he is said to obtain a clear knowledge of his own internal, mental, and bodily state, is enabled to calculate, with accuracy, the phenomena of disease which will naturally and inevitably occur, and to determine what are their most appropriate and effectual remedies. He is also said to possess the same power of internal inspection with regard to other persons who have been placed in magnetic connexion with him. From this fifth degree all the subsequent magnetic states are comprehended under the denomination of *lucidity* or *lucid vision.*

" In the *sixth* degree, the *lucid vision*, which the patient possessed in the former degree, extends to all objects, near and at a distance, in space and time; hence it has been called the degree of *universal* lucidity, commonly called clairvoyance.

" No patient, it is said, can reach the higher degrees of magnetism, without having previously passed through the lower. Individuals, it is true, are sometimes placed in the higher degrees at the first magnetic treatment; but they are supposed to have previously passed through the intermediate states in so rapid a manner as rendered it difficult, or impossible, to distinguish the transactions. External as well as internal influences, not yet sufficiently ascertained dispose a patient, more or less at particular times, to attain a certain degree; and hence, the magnetic sleep is never permanently the same, but always variable."

Anti-Mesmerist.—You have as yet told me nothing about Phreno-Mesmerism, as you call it, which appears to me something like Phrenology, a downright humbug and delusion, but as you have already almost convinced me that there is some truth in mesmeric phenomena, you will be kind enough to let me know a little about the other branch of your subject, Phreno-Mesmerism.

Mesmerist.—This is a very important branch of the subject, and "like gold, although newly brought out of the mine, certainly not the less genuine." Thousands, there are who were as incredulous about it as you, who have acknowledged its truthfulness, and confessed that it made them believe in Phrenology, a science which opens up a perfect knowledge of the human mind in all its workings, for, as George Combe of Edinburgh justly observes, "Look at Phrenology in France, in Britain, and the United States of America : it already directs lunatic asylums, it presides over education, it mitigates the severity of the criminal law, it assuages religious animosity, it guides the historian, is a beacon light to the physiologist, and already has incorporated its nomenclature with the languages of those countries."

Anti-Mesmerist.—Pray, who discovered Phreno-Mesmerism?

Mesmerist.—Several claim the merit of having been the first to discover Phreno-Mesmerism, amongt whom are the Rev. Roy Sunderland, Doctors Collier and Buchanan, all of them residing at that time in America; the former individual gives a very interesting and ingenious theory upon the subject in a work called the "Magnet," published at New York, which I can only refer you to for full particulars. Dr. Engledue, in an address delivered before the members of the London Phrenological Society, speaks of Phreno-Mesmerism thus:

"The discovery of the magnetic excitation of cerebration, as far as I am aware, was made in this country by my two friends, Messrs. Mansfield and Gardiner. These two gentlemen communicated their experiments to me, and I immediately attempted to excite the cerebral organs of one of my patients, who had been regularly magnetised by me for some time for the cure of disease, exactly the same results were obtained.

"On the 7th October, 1841, Mr. Gardiner, during the magnetic trance of one of his patients, played a few notes on a small musical instrument, the patient kept time by a lateral motion of the head. He then sounded the instrument without attending to harmony, the patient shuddered, and appeared to be distressed. He interrogated her as to the cause of this distress; she replied she was in pain; and when asked where, she placed a finger of each hand on the organ of Time, on the same side. I shall not soon forget the enthusiasm of my friend when he communicated this result to me. An apple falling from a tree suggested to Newton the laws by which countless worlds hold their unvarying course; and the muscular distortion of a human countenance suggested thoughts which will assist in unfolding the great problem in cerebral Physiology. After this experiment, Mr. Mansfield returned to Cambridge, where he became acquainted with a gentleman eighteen years of age, exceedingly susceptible of the magnetic influence. The first intimation he had of the fact, that the magnetiser could excite a cerebral organ, was on the 18th of December, 1841. This patient manifested impaired sense of time. He said, for instance, that he had been in a room half an hour, when he had been there more than two hours, and on another occasion two hours and a half; he would refer to events that had taken place more than half an hour before as if a few minutes had only elapsed. Mr. Mansfield breathed on the organ of Time, and then asked his patient the same question, when he named the exact period.

" The cases of my friends are very interesting, but I think it will be more in accordance with your feelings and wishes, if I confine myself to the relation of my own case.

" The case which I am about to relate is that of a young lady, sixteen years of age, who had been confined to her bed eighteen months; she was magnetised for some time, and during the trance manifested a number of extraordinary phenomena; but I shall confine my relation to experiments on cerebration. The patient, having been placed in the trance, was allowed to remain quiet for a short time. I then simply applied my finger to the organ to be excited, and willed that it should become so. The excitation, in the majority of cases, was instantaneous. Thus the finger applied to Imitation, produced the most splendid mimicry it is possible to conceive. The words and gestures of friends were copied in the most exact manner. Anecdotes which had been forgotten by all the members of the family, were repeated in a way that brought the circumstances instantaneously to their recollection, notwithstanding many years had elapsed. On one occasion the manifestation of the faculty was permitted to continue for half an hour, and was then stopped by a wave of the hand over the organ, without contact. The finger on Wit produced immoderate laughter, checked by a wave of the hand, and reproduced by a touch of the finger. The finger on Colour, caused the patient to see a variety of colours, which she said, was coloured worsted. The finger on Size, caused her to say she saw 'heaps of skeins.' When asked the supposed weight of the quantity, she replied she did not know. The finger on the organ of Weight, caused her immediately to exclaim 'hundreds of pounds.' Self-esteem, Firmness, Veneration, Benevolence, Philoprogenitiveness, Caution, &c. &c., were all excited with corresponding results. The natural language of each faculty was most beautiful, and the patient in the natural state could not manifest the functions in any similar degree."

Since this grand discovery was made, the subject has occupied the attention of a vast number of gentlemen, both in public and private; but, at this far advanced state of the science, the names are too numerous to give here. Among the many we may mention Dr. Elliotson, Mr. Braid, Mr. Spencer T. Hall, author of the Phreno-Magnet, &c., the author of the present treatise; Mr. Atkinson, Mr. Brooks, Mr. Simpson, Advocate, Edinburgh; G. C. Holland, M. D., C. Thompson, M. D., D. M'Taggart, Ph. D., &c. &c.

Anti-Mesmerist.—Can you give me any theory of the excitation of the cerebral organs, when a person is under the influence of the mesmeric sleep, or rather your views upon this subject?

Mesmerist.—As I am always anxious to furnish as much information to inquiring minds as possible, I will now proceed to give you a few hints on this topic, in order that you may fully investigate it; for this I conceive to be the duty of all Mesmerists, and Phreno-Mesmerists. Before however, you can understand what I mean, it will be necessary to connect Mesmerism and Phreno-Mesmerism, and shew the relation which one bears to the other. To make you comprehend this, I commence by observing, that a subtle animal fluid is, in my opinion, the principal agent for the production of both. The precise nature of this fluid I cannot define, but I can make my meaning intelligible by comparing it to properties long recognised in other bodies, if not well understood. You, no doubt, are aware, that a certain kind of mineral has been discovered, in various parts of the world, which has been found

to contain or possess several singular and astonishing properties; one of the first of these is attraction, or the power of
drawing other bodies to it. But long after the discovery of this
property, this mineral or magnet was found to possess another,
and very remarkable property, namely, polarity; a third property of the magnet is, its communicativeness, or the power of
imparting the same virtue to another body which it possesses
itself; and it is presumed that there is an analogy between
these properties and the mesmeric phenomena, illustrated in the
power which one individual's mind exercises over that of another, when the latter is either in the vigilant or somnambulic
state; for experience has taught the mesmeriser, that by his
own volition he can cause the mesmerised to think as he thinks,
do as he does, feel as he feels, and, in fact, become all but a part
of himself. There is still another property of the magnet, which
throws a "flood of light" upon the subject, it is that it contains the electric fluid, for this fluid has been obtained from
magnets, and it is a law in nature, that we cannot obtain it
from any object less charged than the body which receives it;
for instance, if an individual receives a spark from the electri-
fying machine, it is because he is less charged than the
machine which imparts the spark. All bodies in an equal
state of electricity are besides known to repel each other, and in
an opposite state to attract each other; so that two bodies con-
taining an equal quantity of this fluid, can never exhibit any
magnetic phenomena by attraction, and we reason from this, that
one person will produce more powerful mesmeric effects than
another—the bilious temperament acting on the nervous—the
sanguine on the lymphatic, and so on; facts, when properly
understood, which will explain how some persons can more
readily induce the magnetic sleep than others. This is a part
of the subject to which the attention of investigators should be
directed, for it must be from a large collection of experiments
and facts, that a rational and philosophical theory of this subject can be formed.

Magnets are made by natural as well as by artificial means;
natural ones are made by the natural operation of the elements acting upon them, for instance, the loadstone, and even
bars of iron, when placed for a long time in certain positions,
acquire the magnetic influence; and as there seem to be
negative and positive properties in nature, states analogous
to mesmeric phenomena may be produced on the human
frame, by the outward action of the elements; and it is thus
that natural somnambulism, trance, catalepsy, paralysis,
epilepsy, &c. &c., may be accounted for. Artificial magnets

are those which are made by the ingenuity of man, a thing that is generally accomplished by friction; experience has taught the Mesmerist that the passes or manipulations produce the magnetic phenomena, so that whether it is the human frame or a piece of iron that is subjected to the influence, no doubt can be entertained that a subtle fluid is the agent. In the one case it enters the pores of the hard steel, and in the other the nervous system; and it will strike every faithful recorder of mesmeric appearances forcibly, that by the very fixing of our eyes and thoughts upon an object for a time, we may attract or concentrate the magnetic fluid in the brain, in the same manner as a piece of steel will attract the lightning from the clouds, which Dr. Franklin fully demonstrated. You are aware, that if you rub tallow into leather the latter becomes soft, and partakes of the nature of that which has been rubbed into it, so we know also, that friction produces the electric fluid, and when that is imparted to other bodies, new and singular properties are conferred on them which they did not before possess. Similar effects may be produced by the mesmeriser upon his patient; the former imparting the magnetic influence to the latter, so as to restore in him the equilibrium of vigour and health. This is borne out by the cases before quoted and by a number of experiments; it is also conformable to reason, for one great principle of electricity is, that as certain as water seeks its own level by the law of gravitation, so certain does the electric fluid seek its equilibrium by the law of attraction. It is known to leave the clouds and fly to the less charged steel rod, and this being the case, will it be too much to assume, that an attracting process is secretly and silently going on between other bodies, though that process may not be apparent or palpable to us? Some of these bodies are endued with the power of attracting more, some less. The fluid is to be found in all that is eaten, drunk, or breathed, and individuals have existed so filled with it that sparks were obtained from their bodies, as vividly as from the Leyden Jar itself. By the great John Hunter this fluid was deemed the vivifying principle, or principle of life. Supposing it to be such, the more equably it is distributed through the organs of the brain and nervous filaments the better; for it must be just in proportion as it is so distributed or present that the mind is raised or depressed. Take the clouds above our heads for an illustration—when they are in a state of equilibrium with regard to the electric fluid, all is calm and beautiful, but when they are oppositely charged, they become disturbed, presenting us occasionally with the appearances of instant destruction, and producing in our minds sadness and awe; thus proving that there is a sympathetic influence existing between them and us, and shewing that we as well as they, being part of the great whole, are composed in some measure of the same elements and subject to the same laws. Descending from great natural operations such as those down to these that are merely artificial, we find that, through the agency of friction, the magnet communicates its properties to hard steel, and this being the fact, is it not rational to think that the human body, when subjected to something of a similar process, should be capable of manifesting analogous phenomena or exhibiting like results?

Anti-Mesmerist.—The theory is plausible, though it may not be true; but without disputing it at present I want to know from you what Phreno-Mesmerism is?

Mesmerist.—You are now in a position to comprehend something of it; Phreno-Mesmerism means nothing more nor less than the excitation of the cerebral organs of a patient, either with or without contact, and producing from him involuntary manifestations which accord with the doctrines of Phrenology, while he is in the vigilant or somnolent state.

Anti-Mesmerist.—What is the difference between these two states?

Mesmerist.—The vigilant state is that in which the patient can see and hear the operator, and know what he is about, but in which he has been so far affected notwithsanding his consciousness, as not to be able to suppress an involuntary manifestation when any of his cerebral organs is touched. The somnolent state is that in which he is deprived of consciousness, and rendered so far oblivious as not to remember what occurred to him in it when aroused. In this state, the different cerebral organs resemble a piano, when excited they give forth manifestations in accordance with Phrenology, unknown to the patient, and entirely of themselves.

Anti-Mesmerist.—How is such an influence attained over the patient, or in what manner is it supposed that these manifestations are produced?

Mesmerist.—At the onset I should tell you, that as there are some persons more susceptible than others of mesmeric influence, so also are there persons more sluggish than others, when in the mesmeric sleep. The difference in this respect arises from the difference of the texture of the various brains, or what is called difference of temperament; nervous and sanguine temperaments for instance, are more vivacious than the lymphatic; and so excitable are persons of the former, that many of them give forth manifestations under a slight touch, or even without contact whereas persons of the latter, often require a pretty smart and continuous pressure on the cerebral organs before the symptoms of feeling are evinced. Be the temperaments, however, of susceptible persons what it may, their whole nervous system is thrown into a very peculiar condition by the induction of the mesmeric sleep; the blood is propelled by the process with greater force to the brain—the pulse quickened, and in certain stages of it there is a great exaltation of the organs of sense: hearing is heightened, smell improved, seeing too—though not through the eyes, is rendered more powerful or perfect; and, it is on this principle of an exaltation of the powers of the organs of sense that many mesmeric phenomena are accounted for, such as returning articles to the various persons from whom they had been taken by the patient, while in the unconscious state—not to mention clairvoyance itself.

Anti-Mesmerist.—How do you distinguish between the conscious and the unconscious state.

Mesmerist.—They are easily distinguishable, one should think; the conscious state may be said to be that in which the whole brain is at work; the unconscious, that in which the whole brain is benumbed or asleep; an individual, while his brain is in the former state, can be so excited by several artificial means, independent of the mesmeric one, as to be deprived of self-control; while an individual in the latter state must, if a manifestation is required, be either roused up to full consciousness as from a common sleep, or must have, as by the Phreno-mesmeric process, certain organs stimulated into activity, while all the other organs are dormant or at rest.

Anti-Mesmerist.—But how are the cerebral organs stimulated, or brought into activity, by the touch?

Mesmerist.—If the whole human frame can be reduced to a state of perfect obliviousness by the mesmeric process, which few persons at this time of day can deny, and none can disprove, and if consciousness can again be restored, may we not as readily demesmerise a single cerebral organ, or stimulate it to activity, as an arm or leg, or operate on the root of the nervous system as readily as on the different parts or poles of the body to which that system extends? You may be aware that certain substances placed upon the surface of other bodies, will render them impervious to the action of external agents, in like manner, perhaps, the brain may be rendered unconscious to the external world, by the addition of an external or the repulsion of an internal magnetic fluid, and the contact of a body in an opposite state may produce an action analogous to an electric shock, arousing the organs from their dormant state to more than their ordinary activity; and hence it may be that the mind is stirred, or that phreno-mesmeric manifestations are produced.

Every modern physiologist admits the brain to be the organ of the mind; Phrenologists go farther, and call it a congeries of organs—and the Phreno-Mesmerists go still farther, for they prove the Phrenologist right. The connexion, however, between the nerves and the different cerebral organs is not well understood. A medical friend with whom I correspond, informs me that he has repeatedly counted the filaments composing a nerve, and has found the number to correspond in a very remarkable manner with the number of organs contained in the brain, and in this way he endeavours to shew that each filament performs a distinct function in the grand arrangement of sensation and motion, and that we may with equal propriety say, we have a nerve of benevolence, a nerve of veneration, a nerve of self-esteem, a nerve of combativeness, a nerve of destructiveness, a nerve of music or tune, and time; each filament being the nervous agent of a cerebral organ or mental faculty. This may appear somewhat reasonable to all mesmerists, for by the excitation of the poles located at the outer angles of the mouth, and in various parts of the face, we can produce manifestations similar to those produced by the excitement of the cerebral organs themselves. From my own experience, I infer that every feeling or emotion of the mind has its distinct nerve of communication from the brain to the face, for it is as rational to suppose this, as that we have nerves of sensation and motion, a fact recently demonstrated by Charles Bell. If this theory were established, it would cause the physiognomist and phrenologist to be united, and at once explain how the mind of man looks out in the face, under the emotions of love, anger, fear, veneration, adhesiveness, self-esteem, and love of approbation.

Anti-Mesmerist.—Do you contend that it requires the same conductors or non-conductors as electricity, to magnetise or demagnetise the cerebral organs of a mesmeric patient, when under the mesmeric influence.

Mesmerist.—I by no means argue in that manner. The fluid of Animal Magnetism may be more subtle still than ordinary electric fluid. The principle, though existing, is not yet perfectly understood. No doubt it has laws by which it is governed, but they are not yet discovered, nor will this be

a matter of surprise, when it is remembered that the planet-
ary system moved with as exact regularity for thousands of
years before the great Newton's time as now, though no one
knew how it was moved. In like manner Phreno-Mesmerism
may require as gigantic a mind to reduce it to a proper system. I do not urge my theory as true, but mention it as pro-
bable, and as you wished me to give you a few ideas of my
my own, perhaps they may not be lost on you and other in-
quirers into the phenomena of Phreno-Mesmerism.

Anti-Mesmerist.—Is it possible to excite the cerebral organs,
when a person is in a state of vigilance, by pressure?

Mesmerist.—The compiler of this treatise has done that
often on very nervous patients; one case in particular was
met with at Rochdale, in England, where a youth about sixteen years of age, of a nervo-sanguine temperament, and highly
excitable, manifested all the phrenological organs when awake
under a slight pressure, and could exercise no power of resis-
tance. A number of cases can be adduced from Mr. Spencer
T. Hall's Phreno Magnet, and other mesmeric works, all cor-
roborative of the above fact.

Anti-Mesmerist.—Can you furnish me with any well authenticated cases of Phreno-Mesmerism?

Mesmerist.—This being a mere conversazione, I cannot enter in full, even into my own theory and cases, much less the
cases of others, so I must refer you to the Zoist, Phreno-Magnet, The Edinburgh Phrenological Journal, &c. &c.

Anti-Mesmerist.—You have said a good deal about a fluid,
now can you give me any respectable authority, who advocated
the existence of a magnetic fluid in the animal body?

Mesmerist.—The opinion of Dr. Bell ought not to be over-
looked, as I do consider it worthy of some attention. " There
is," says he, " an universal fluid which fills all space; every
body is endowed with a certain quantity of electric fluid; there
exists an attraction or sympathy and antipathy between animated bodies.

" The universal currents of the universal fluids are the cause
and existence of bodies; one may accelerate those currents in
a body, and produce crisis and somnambulism, which is done
by acting reciprocally upon one another, by increasing
the currents going across the pores, in consequence of the
absolute will of the operator; as there exists a general and reciprocal gravitation of all celestial bodies towards each other,
so there exists a particular and reciprocal gravitation of the
earth towards the whole, and that whole towards each of its
parts. The reciprocal action of all bodies is operated upon by

the universal insensible perspiration, or vapour, flowing in and out, as you see in a real loadstone, or an artificial magnet, forming an outside atmosphere; it also produces currents in a more or less degree, according to the analogy of bodies, and this we can observe, that when two individuals are placed opposite to each other, the one attracts, and the other repels." So far for Doctor Bell; besides his theory, I will give you the opinions of several scientific men, taken from a work on Mesmerism.

The first is that of the celebrated Cuvier, who fully admits the truth of Mesmerism, and says: "We must confess that it is very difficult, in the experiments which have for their object, the action which the nervous system of different individuals can exercise one upon another, to distinguish the effect of the imagination of the individual upon whom the experiment is tried, from the physical results produced by persons who act for him. The effects, however, ignorant of the agency, and upon individuals whom the operation has deprived of consciousness, and those which animals present, do not permit us to doubt that the proximity of two animated bodies in certain positions, combined with certain movements, have a real effect, independently of all participation of the fancy; it appears also clearly, that these effects arise from some nervous communication which is established between their nervous systems.

Dr. Joseph Gall, the founder of Phrenology, says: "It being, however, impossible to deny such facts of Mesmerism as occur in some nervous diseases, are they to be ascribed to mere imagination, an excitement of the feelings by the gesticulation and proximity of the manipulator, or to the operation of an unknown power?" Gall admits this power, and even does not reject the hypothesis of its connexion with a fluid. "How often," says he, "in intoxication, hysterical and hypochondrical attacks, convulsions, fevers, and insanity, under violent emotions, after long fasting, through the effects of such poisons as opium, hemlock, &c., are we not, in some measure, transferred into perfectly different beings, for instance, into poets, actors, &c. Just as in dreaming, the thoughts frequently have more delicacy, and the sensations are more acute, and we can hear and answer just as in ordinary somnambulism, we can rise, walk, see with our eyes shut, touch with our hands, &c., so we allow that similar phenomena may take place in artificial somnambulism, and in a higher degree. We acknowledge a fluid which has an especial affinity with the nervous system, which can emanate from an individual, pass into another, and accumulate in virtue of particular affinities, more in certain parts than others; we admit the existence of a fluid, the sub-traction of which lessens, and the accumulation augments the power of the nerves; which places one part of the nervous system in repose, and heightens the activity of another, which, therefore, may produce an artificial somnambulism."

Anti-Mesmerist.—You say that Colquhoun, in his work on Mesmerism, mentions the fifth and sixth degrees, or stages of sleep, are those stages which are commonly called the clairvoy-ant stages.

Mesmerist.—I understand him to mean as much, and if I am to believe the evidence of my own senses, and the testi-mony of several highly respectable and intelligent individuals, as well as Colquhoun, I must conclude that clairvoyance is a true and natural phenomena; in fact, it has been witnessed by so many persons, and in nearly all parts of the world, that to deny it, even if I had not seen it, would be the height of incre-dulity on my part. I could, however, adduce many cases in cor-roboration of Colquhoun's statements. One case came under my notice, when lecturing at Newcastle-on-Tyne. A respectable gentleman, and partner in a bookbinding and paper ruling establishment there, having been very sceptical on the subject of Mesmerism in its commonest form, took upon himself to ridicule the whole system as a farce, and the advocates of it as impostors; however, being induced to submit to the opera-tion, he was, after considerable labour and many trials, over-come, and the phenomena brought out to the astonishment and admiration of a number of his friends, whom he had invited as witnesses to see fair play. In the sleep he was perfectly able to tell what any article was when held over his head or behind his back, with as apparent ease as if his eyes were open, though they were shut the whole time of the experi-ment, and in every instance he was correct. When a watch was held over his head, or behind his back, he told what it was, with handkerchiefs the same, both describing the pattern and colour, also wafers of all sizes and colours were tried, which he named correctly in every instance, and the most astonish-ing part of all was, he was able to repeat every thing he had seen and told in his mesmeric state when quite awake.

A cure of a somewhat remarkable nature was also witnessed at Sheffield, where a young lady on whom magnetic somnam-bulism was very soon induced by the compiler of this little work, called darkness light, and light darkness, and could see better in the darkness than when it was light; she was able to distinguish any person in a dark room with the eyes closed, nd could not do so when the gas was lighted ; she was labouring under a disease of the spine, for which she was mesmerised upwards of eighty times, and with great success.* She was able to tell, for several days before, when she would walk, and did so to a minute; was able to tell the Mesmeriser's thoughts, and told the taste of any article put into his mouth. More could be recorded of this case, but the few facts which are now stated will be sufficient to warrant the belief in a power of a more extraordinary nature than yet dreamed of by the bulk of mankind, and which may one day throw a new light on many subjects yet dark and mysterious in their appearance.

Other cases in corroboration of Phreno-Mesmerism and clairvoyance, which came under the Author's own management in various part of England, Scotland, and Ireland, are worthy of insertion here. They are not added for the purpose of proving him more successful as an experimentalist than others engaged in the same great field of nature, but because they may tend to promote the science of which he is an ardent advocate. A description of those cases he will not give so much in his own words as in the language of those who witnessed them.

The following extract is from the *Kelso Chronicle*, of April 28th, 1843:

" On Wednesday evening the proofs of the science of Phreno-Mesmerism arose to complete demonstration. It was a *mesmeric Pentecost*, hundreds were made converts. The house on the occasion was quite insufficient to give accommodation to the wondering throng. Among the subjects operated upon was a painter, ignorant of the science of Phrenology, and incapable of entering into any collusion with the lecturer to deceive the audience. This person gave out, during the mesmeric sleep, the same manifestations as the lecturer's own subjects; firmly proving to all who believed the testimony of their senses, that Phreno-Magnetism stands on an imperishable basis. And, to give one proof more of the science, Dr. Lee mesmerised an individual in a private room, after the dismissal of Mr. Adair's lecture, in presence of three or four gentlemen, amongst whom was the writer of this article, and Messrs. W. and G. Wilson. This case was by far the most brilliant triumph of the truth of this inexplicable science. After the mass of irrefragable evidence, all doubts or

---

* The name and address will be furnished by Mr. Adair, to any person labouring under a similar complaint, and he would recommend Mesmerism in every case of this nature.

disputations about the truth of Phrenology are set at rest, and the analysis of the brain completely established; this grand physiological discovery is one of the countless victories that the student of nature is always achieving; long may Mr. Adair go on in his splendid course, and long may a discerning public reward him with their patronage!

" In corroboration of the above report, Mr. Adair, was presented with a testimonial to the same effect, which is here subjoined, and from gentlemen of high respectability, who, at Mr. Adair's early lectures were the most determined sceptics and opponents he had to contend against: ' We, the undersigned individuals, have attended Mr. Adair's experimental lectures on Phreno-Mesmerism, and have no hesitation in bearing testimony to the tangible and incontrovertible evidence which he has produced in support of the science. His successful experiments on our townsmen, of unquestionable veracity, leave no room for doubt or disputation on the matter, and entitle him to the candid hearing of a discerning public.—W. TURNBULL, Magistrate; W. SCOTT, Magistrate, JAMES LEE, M.D., JOHN BLYTH, M.D., W. WILSON, Orchard House, Hawick, April 20th, 1843.'"

EXTRACT FROM THE LIVERPOOL MERCURY OF JULY 7th, 1843.

" Mr. Adair, in obedience with a former declaration, then proposed that a galvanic shock should be tried upon the arm of the young woman (Miss Watson), when in the rigid state, in order to prove that there was no physical effort in maintaining such rigidity. A medical gentleman volunteered that it should first be tried upon his arm when in its natural state; the result of which was, that he could not withstand the shock; the same power was immediately applied to the patient, when not a muscle relaxed in the slightest degree."

From the *Sheffield and Rotherham Independent*, Nov. 11th, 1844: " the most striking characteristics of Mr. Adair's experiments, were the attitudes assumed by the young female, which were of the most astonishing description we have yet witnessed."

EXTRACT OF A LETTER FROM THE LIVERPOOL CHRONICLE, ON PHRENO-MESMERISM.

To the Editor.

" SIR,—The great excitement which has prevailed, and still continues to exist, respecting the truth of the phreno-mesmeric

E

experiments which have been so repeatedly brought before the public, has induced me to investigate the subject fully, by the following series of experiments, which I deem myself justified in submitting to the public, in order to convince them, if possible, of the truth of a science which may prove beneficial to the interests and well-being of society. On the 23rd of May last, I was first put into the mesmeric sleep by a friend. I could not open my eyes, but was perfectly conscious; he again put me into the sleep on the 29th, when the results were similar. I suspended my experiments from that time to last Saturday evening, when Mr. Adair, of Sheffield, succeeded in putting me into the sleep. On the following day he again put me into the sleep: produced catalepsy in the arms, but I was still in a conscious state; he then, according to the testimony of several respectable individuals who were present, brought out manifestations of several of the cerebral organs, of which I had not the slightest recollection, thereby convincing them of the candour and honesty of the experiments. The next evening, out of justice to Mr. Adair, I allowed him to put me into a sleep before the audience, at his lecture, when similar results to those obtained the previous day were obtained.

"The above are striking facts, which convinced me, and several respectable inhabitants of this town, that there is not any occasion for collusion between the operator and patient in these cases; but that the effects may and have been produced, as in the present instance, in a fair and candid manner. Your insertion of the above, in your earliest publication, will greatly oblige,

"Your's, truly,

"GODFREY LEVI.

"17, *Brownlow-hill, June* 30, 1843."

Since the above letter was sent for publication, Mr. Adair has had occasion to visit Liverpool, and being anxious to see as many of his well-wishers as possible, called upon Godfrey Levi, when he then informed him that previously to his having been mesmerised he suffered dreadfully from headach and a giddiness, which often prevented him from doing his work in a proper manner, but now, and ever since he last submitted to Mesmerism, he was quite well, and perfectly free from headach and the dizziness which he was formerly liable to.

EXTRACT FROM THE PEOPLE'S PHRENOLOGICAL JOURNAL,
LONDON.

" *Carlisle—Mesmeric Phrenology.*—Mr. Adair, of Sheffield,
has not a little excited the '*wonder*' of the inhabitants of our
city, by a series of lectures and experiments during the last
week, elucidatory of the new science of Mesmero-Phrenology;
and the results are truly surprising. He was accompanied by
a young man and woman, upon whom he operated with such
perfect success, and so clearly demonstrated the truths of
Phrenology, as at once to give rise to suspicion of collusion, and
the greatest scepticism for awhile prevailed. It is worthy of
remark, that the greatest hostility was shewn by the worthy
sons of Esculapius, some of whom behaved scarcely with common decency at the early meetings. Mr. Adair has, however,
triumphed over all opposition, and established the science be-
yond dispute, by his successful operations upon several of the
natives of our city; scepticism is now completely silenced;
men must believe according to the strongest amount of evidence presented to their senses; and even our profound M. D.'s.
are obliged to admit ' there are more things than are dreamt
of in their philosophy.'

" You will not have space for any of the details. Mr. Adair,
though (as he says) not much of a lecturer, is a most skilful
manipulator, and called forth the phrenological manifestations
most beautifully, and in such a manner as to leave not a doubt
upon the minds of the audience, of the great truth of the prin-
ciples of Phrenology. We read much of a multiplicity of new
organs, said to have been discovered through the medium of
the magnetic sleep, but Mr. Adair does not seem to recognize
the existence of any of them; there is one, however, which
would seem to be well established, that of ' terror,' under
the influence of which all the subjects tried exhibited most
lively symptoms, starting back, and trembling in every limb.
The *clairvoyant* state was produced in two or three individuals; and certainly not the least astonishing of the whole
proceedings was the recognition of a watch placed above the
crown of the head, and the discernment of colours when placed
behind the back. Various private parties here have tried
Mesmerism with the greatest success; sceptics have alike operated and been operated upon; and with the production of
such astonishing phenomena, it is impossible the public mind
can rest. Even to those who formerly opposed Phrenology, it

offers indisputable evidence of its truth; let phrenologists consider it worthy of their deepest investigation, and, depend upon
it, their labour will not be in vain.   Should this investigation
lead to any particular result in our city, you may rely upon
its being communicated to your valuable Journal.

" Your's, respectfully,

" S. H."

CONCLUSION.

Within the last three years, the Author of this treatise has
delivered Experimental Lectures on Mesmerism and Phreno-
Mesmerism, in Doncaster, Halifax, Dewsbury, Bradford, Reigh-
ley, Skipton, Carlisle, Wigtown (England), Hawick, Kelso,
Newcastle-on-Tyne, South and North Shields, Settle, Lancas-
ter, Liverpool, Whitehaven, Dumfries, Castledouglass, Kirk-
cudbright, Creetown (his native town), Wigtown (Scotland), Newtownstewart, Garliestown, Whitehorn, Sheffield,
Rotherham, Thorn, Hull, Barton, Beverley, Cleckheaton,
Worksop, Ashton, Oldham, Rochdale, Haywood, Bury, Bake-
well, Buxton, Macclesfield, Congleton, Sandback, Chester,
Crew, Nantwich, Middlewich, Douglas and Ramsay, Isle of
Man, Dublin and Kingstown; in every one of these places he
met with individuals on whom the mesmeric and phreno-mesmeric sleep were produced.

The favourable notices of his Lectures which appeared in the
Dublin newspapers during his three months' stay in that city,
where he lectured and experimented for upwards of sixty even-
ings in the Rotunda, are so numerous that he could not think of
quoting in this little work more than one or two of them, which
he selects on account of their brevity.   Among those he is
necessitated to exclude are two letters speaking very flatter-
ingly of him, from Henry Grattan Curran, Esq., an eminent
Barrister, and son of the late John Philpot Curran, the celebrated Irish orator.   Besides his public lectures in Dublin,
the writer had several private *seances* at his own residence,
which were attended by numbers of the Nobility and Gentry,
and their Ladies; among his auditors were the Lord Adair,
Sir Philip Crampton, Judge Crampton, Sir Henry Meredith,
Bart., Arthur Bushe, Esq., son of the late Lord Chief Justice
Bushe, Doctor Spratt, D.D., Smith O'Brien, Esq., M. P., James
Haughton, Esq., Doctor Little, &c. &c.

The following are the notices alluded to above, taken from *The Pilot* Newspaper:

"Phreno-Mesmerism appears now to be established as a reality, not a fiction, in Dublin, for the lectures and illustrations of Mr. Adair, at the Rotunda, are nightly frequented by crowded and fashionable audiences; his success in producing the sleep, and bringing out the phrenological manifestations, on residents of this city, who were previously strangers to him, has removed the scepticism as to the truth of the science that prevailed with regard to it, so long as the operations were confined to his own subjects. One young man, named Thompson, a cabinet-maker, well known in Dublin, has been operated on several times, and has exhibited more extraordinary phenomena than Mr. Adair deemed it advisable to produce before a sceptical audience from the persons who travel with him; his power over the young man in the waking state was most extraordinary; he not only nailed him with a few passes of his hand to the platform, but compelled him to raise his arms, extend them in a horizontal position, put them down, shake his head, and fall even in obedience to his will, or in imitation of his movements. This, he alleges, is produced by the influence of mind on mind; but, if it be, all that we can say with regard to it is, that it is a most astonishing influence.

"On Wednesday night the lecture of Mr. Adair attained an increase of interest from the fact of a young lady, a native of this city, whom the lecturer had seen but a few hours before, being subjected to a trial of the mesmeric influence. The experiment was eminently successful, and elicited some exceedingly interesting manifestations. On touching the various organs the actions natural to each were excited in a most striking degree, and a most beautiful instance of the fidelity with which the manipulation of the operator was obeyed occurred in the case of the organ of Veneration. The attitude was nature—Catholic nature, &c."

"PHRENO-MESMERISM.

"A private *seance* of the friends of Mesmerism, to which quite an aristocratic circle of visitors came by invitation, took place at Mr. Adair's own residence on Thursday evening. Five persons were mesmerised on the occasion, four of whom are respectable citizens of Dublin, who permitted themselves to be operated upon there, but who would, of course, have a disin-

clination to appear on a public platform.   Sir Philip Crampton, the Surgeon-General, was present among the visitors for
a part of the sitting.   The subject is acquiring strength here,
and is moving in far higher circles now than when Surgeon
Mathias and Doctor King made their feeble, but abortive, efforts
to strangle it.   Touching the course pursued by the latter
gentleman and the editors of the *Dublin Medical Press* towards
Mr. Adair, the writer of the present notice deems it his duty
to make an observation.   In that paper a letter signed ' Charles
Croker King, M. D.,' appeared on the 24th September.   It
purported to give a description of what occurred at two mesmeric lectures which the Doctor witnessed, but contained in
reality a most strange misrepresentation of what took place, and
stigmatised besides Mr. Adair as a charlatan and a cheat, his
auditors as dupes, and his subjects as mere knavish impostors.
The writer of the present notice happened to be present at both
of the lectures.   Seeing Mr. King's letter—knowing, too, how
far his assertions devaricated from truth—he thought it right
to contradict them, and wrote to the editors of the *Medical
Press* for the purpose, giving his name and address, and refer-
ring these gentlemen to a host of witnesses for the accuracy of
his statements.   But, though they published the slander, they
refused to insert its refutation—a thing not very usual with
newspaper proprietors.   Other steps would, in consequence of
this refusal, have been taken to defeat the object of Mr. King,
had not that gentleman, though a lecturer at one of the medical
schools, been found on inquiry not to occupy so high a place in
his Profession as would render him worthy of too much notice."

Pilot, October 10, 1845.

THE END.